*The God Really Loves You Book Series™ Presents:*

# GOD
# Really
# Loves You
## and
# He Helps You Choose!

**Written and Illustrated
by Wendy Nelson**

*God Really Loves You Book Series™ presents:*

# GOD Really Loves You
## and He Helps You Choose!

Text Copyright ©2023 by Wendy Nelson
Artwork Copyright ©2023 by Wendy Nelson

Published by MediaTek Grafx
POB 62, Bonnieville, Kentucky, 42713

ISBN 978-1-0880-6989-9

Design and production by MediaTek Grafx, Bonnieville, Kentucky
Special thanks to Joan Swan for loving review, critique and advice

The Publisher has made every effort to avoid errors or omissions. Opinions, stories, and themes are intended for entertainment, motivation for research and future study. This book includes content that is non-fiction.

All Scripture quotations are from the The Holy Bible, King James Version, Pradis Software Rel 02.04.03, Built with Conform Version 5.00.0051, Version 5.1.50 Copyright ©2002 The Zondervan Corporation All Rights Reserved.

All rights reserved. This Publication may not be reproduced in whole or in part, stored or transmitted by any means. Media may use small portions for reviews. Please request written permission from Publisher for any other reason.

Printed in the United States of America

*A Special Gift for*

_____

*From*

_____

*Note*

_____

_____

_____

*Date*

_____

God
really loves you!
God is your Father
in Heaven.

He loves you
this much!

God gave you the Bible,
to show you how to live,
and to tell you about
His Son, Jesus.

The Bible is the story of
God's love for you!

*1 John 4:19 We love him, because he first loved us.*

*1 John 3:1 Behold, what manner of love the Father hath bestowed upon us, that we should be called the sons of God: therefore the world knoweth us not, because it knew him not.*

God is holy and special. He is three persons in one:

God the Father, God the Son, Jesus, and God the Holy Spirit.

*Matthew 28:19-20 Go ye therefore, and teach all nations, baptizing them in the name of the Father, and of the Son, and of the Holy Ghost: 20 Teaching them to observe all things whatsoever I have commanded you: and, lo, I am with you alway, even unto the end of the world. Amen.*

God helps you make choices in life. He gives you His Word in the Bible, to teach you!

Study God's Word.

Choose to trust and love God more than anything or anyone else, instead of rejecting Him.

*Proverbs 3:5-6 Trust in the Lord with all thine heart; and lean not unto thine own understanding. In all thy ways acknowledge him, and he shall direct thy paths.*

*1 John 2:15 Love not the world, neither the things that are in the world. If any man love the world, the love of the Father is not in him.*

*Hebrews 13:5-6 Let your conversation be without covetousness; and be content with such things as ye have: for he hath said, I will never leave thee, nor forsake thee. So that we may boldly say, The Lord is my helper, and I will not fear what man shall do unto me.*

Jesus taught us how to choose.

Choose to love, instead of hate.

Choose to forgive, instead of having a resentment.

*Matthew 18:15 Moreover if thy brother shall trespass against thee, go and tell him his fault between thee and him alone: if he shall hear thee, thou hast gained thy brother.*

*Ephesians 4:32 And be ye kind one to another, tender-hearted, forgiving one another, even as God for Christ's sake hath forgiven you.*

*Matthew 7:12 Therefore all things whatsoever ye would that men should do to you, do ye even so to them: for this is the law and the prophets.*

Choose not to sin and to be good,
instead of choosing to sin,
which is doing or saying very bad things.

Obey God and be strong. Choose to do good
and not bad, even if friends pressure you.

*1 John 2:1 My little children, these things write I unto you,
that ye sin not. And if any man sin, we have an advocate
with the Father, Jesus Christ the righteous:*

*1 Corinthians 15:34 Awake to righteousness, and sin not;
for some have not the knowledge of God:
I speak this to your shame.*

*Romans 12:2 And be not conformed to this world:
but be ye transformed by the renewing of your mind,
that ye may prove what is that good, and acceptable,
and perfect, will of God.*

A sin is something we do against God and what He teaches us to do.

God sent His Son, Jesus, to pay for our sins on the cross.

If we pray that we are sorry for our sin, and we accept Jesus as our Savior, we are saved and go to heaven when we die.

Do you feel sorry after you do something bad? If you are sorry and promise not to do the bad thing again, it is called repenting. We talk to God and we repent of all sin.

*2 Peter 3:9 The Lord is not slack concerning his promise, as some men count slackness; but is longsuffering to us-ward, not willing that any should perish, but that all should come to repentance.*

*John 3:16-17 For God so loved the world, that he gave his only begotten Son, that whosoever believeth in him should not perish, but have everlasting life. 17 For God sent not his Son into the world to condemn the world; but that the world through him might be saved.*

After Jesus paid the price for our sins,
He went to Heaven to be with God.

God sent the Holy Spirit in Jesus' name.

The Holy Spirit is our comforter, and He helps you remember everything Jesus taught.

Jesus said not to worry or to be afraid.
The Holy Spirit gives you peace from Jesus.

*John 14:26-27 But the Comforter, which is the Holy Ghost, whom the Father will send in my name, he shall teach you all things, and bring all things to your remembrance, whatsoever I have said unto you. 27 Peace I leave with you, my peace I give unto you: not as the world giveth, give I unto you. Let not your heart be troubled, neither let it be afraid.*

Choose to be thankful and to pray to God, instead of worrying.

Choose to follow Jesus and His example, instead of rejecting Him.

You can be happy and feel peace! God has great things planned for your future!

*Philippians 4:6-7 Be careful for nothing; but in every thing by prayer and supplication with thanksgiving let your requests be made known unto God. And the peace of God, which passeth all understanding, shall keep your hearts and minds through Christ Jesus.*

*1 Peter 2:21 For even hereunto were ye called: because Christ also suffered for us, leaving us an example, that ye should follow his steps:*

*John 8:12 Then spake Jesus again unto them, saying, I am the light of the world: he that followeth me shall not walk in darkness, but shall have the light of life.*

Choose to honor and obey your parents, and tell them important things, instead of disrespecting them and rebelling, or keeping secrets!

*Exodus 20:12 Honour thy father and thy mother: that thy days may be long upon the land which the Lord thy God giveth thee.*

*Ephesians 6:1-2 Children, obey your parents in the Lord: for this is right. Honour thy father and mother; (which is the first commandment with promise;)*

*Luke 8:17 For nothing is secret, that shall not be made manifest; neither any thing hid, that shall not be known and come abroad.*

*Proverbs 4:1-2 Hear, ye children, the instruction of a father, and attend to know understanding. For I give you good doctrine, forsake ye not my law.*

Choose to pay attention, instead of ignoring.

Listen to advice.

Obey good parents who love you.

Pray about everything.

Choose to learn important lessons and love God, instead of being unwise and loving money more than God.

*Proverbs 16:20 He that handleth a matter wisely shall find good: and whoso trusteth in the Lord, happy is he.*

*Matthew 6:24 No man can serve two masters: for either he will hate the one, and love the other; or else he will hold to the one, and despise the other. Ye cannot serve God and mammon.*

*Proverbs 22:6-7 Train up a child in the way he should go: and when he is old, he will not depart from it. The rich ruleth over the poor, and the borrower is servant to the lender.*

God wants you to see the good things
He made for you!
Appreciate all of creation.
When you get older, you will work hard,
eat healthy food,
enjoy good drinks, and be happy!

Choose to eat the healthy
fruits, bread, and carrots,
instead of too much candy
or too many cookies!

Proverbs 25:27-28 *It is not good to eat much honey:
so for men to search their own glory is not glory.
He that hath no rule over his own spirit
is like a city that is broken down, and without walls.*

Ecclesiastes 8:15 *Then I commended mirth, because a
man hath no better thing under the sun, than to eat, and to
drink, and to be merry: for that shall abide with him
of his labour the days of his life,
which God giveth him under the sun.*

Choose to be a good helper,
instead of being lazy.

When we choose to be good,
God is happy for us.
We look for the good things and we feel good.
We smile a lot!

*2 Thessalonians 3:10-12 For even when we were with you, this we commanded you, that if any would not work, neither should he eat. For we hear that there are some which walk among you disorderly, working not at all, but are busybodies. Now them that are such we command and exhort by our Lord Jesus Christ, that with quietness they work, and eat their own bread.*

*Colossians 3:23-24 And whatsoever ye do, do it heartily, as to the Lord, and not unto men; Knowing that of the Lord ye shall receive the reward of the inheritance: for ye serve the Lord Christ.*

Choose good friends,
instead of kids who have bad behavior.

Share some popcorn!

Choose to be friends with people who love Jesus, instead of being friends with angry people. Choose to love enemies, and pray for them, instead of getting revenge.

*Proverbs 22:24-25 Make no friendship with an angry man; and with a furious man thou shalt not go:*
*Lest thou learn his ways, and get a snare to thy soul.*

*Romans 12:19 Dearly beloved, avenge not yourselves, but rather give place unto wrath: for it is written, Vengeance is mine; I will repay, saith the Lord.*

*Luke 6:35 But love ye your enemies, and do good, and lend, hoping for nothing again; and your reward shall be great, and ye shall be the children of the Highest: for he is kind unto the unthankful and to the evil.*

Choose to say "no"
and to walk away from bad situations,
instead of joining in with the kids
doing bad things.

Be brave!

*Romans 16:17 Now I beseech you, brethren, mark them which cause divisions and offences contrary to the doctrine which ye have learned; and avoid them.*

*1 Corinthians 10:13 There hath no temptation taken you but such as is common to man: but God is faithful, who will not suffer you to be tempted above that ye are able; but will with the temptation also make a way to escape, that ye may be able to bear it.*

*2 Timothy 1:7 For God hath not given us the spirit of fear; but of power, and of love, and of a sound mind.*

Sometimes, we make bad choices.
A bad choice to sin
will have consequences.
We might feel sad, we might get punished,
or some sin can even lead to death.

If we are angry,
we might respond
in a bad way.
If we have
hurt feelings,
we might lash out
at others.

If we are afraid,
we might say or do
something bad.

*1 John 1:9 If we confess our sins, he is faithful and just to forgive us our sins, and to cleanse us from all unrighteousness.*

*Romans 6:23 For the wages of sin is death; but the gift of God is eternal life through Jesus Christ our Lord.*

Choose to be wise and discern truth, instead of being foolish and being deceived.

You may feel the Holy Spirit help you and guide you.

*1 John 4:1 Beloved, believe not every spirit, but try the spirits whether they are of God: because many false prophets are gone out into the world.*

*1 John 3:7 Little children, let no man deceive you: he that doeth righteousness is righteous, even as he is righteous.*

*James 1:19 Wherefore, my beloved brethren, let every man be swift to hear, slow to speak, slow to wrath:*

*Proverbs 18:15 The heart of the prudent getteth knowledge; and the ear of the wise seeketh knowledge.*

**Good morning, God!**

Life can be easy or life can be difficult.
We must have tools to handle adversity.

Today is a good day,
but bad things can happen.
A lot of people are good,
but they can do bad things.

Tomorrow is a new day,
so pray to God about everything,
and things will get better!
Choose to wake up with a smile,
instead of a frown!

Lamentations 3:22-23 It is of the Lord's mercies that we are not consumed, because his compassions fail not. They are new every morning: great is thy faithfulness.

Psalms 118:24 This is the day which the Lord hath made; we will rejoice and be glad in it.

Psalms 5:3 My voice shalt thou hear in the morning, O Lord; in the morning will I direct my prayer unto thee, and will look up.

What could you choose to do,
if you are angry, upset, have hurt feelings,
feel jealous, or are worrying about something?

| **READ** the Bible | **TELL** mom and dad | **CUDDLE** your cat |
|---|---|---|
| **PET** your dog | **KNOW** God loves you | **PRAY** to God about it |
| **WALK** away | **SHARE** feelings | **COLOR** a picture |
| **PLAY** with toys | **WATCH** the birds | **COUNT** to 10 |
| **BE** thankful | **HELP** mom or dad | **TALK** to sister |
| **TALK** to brother | **BE** strong | **SMELL** flowers |

God loves us. We become stronger when we endure hardships.

*John 16:33 These things I have spoken unto you, that in me ye might have peace. In the world ye shall have tribulation: but be of good cheer; I have overcome the world.*

*2 Corinthians 12:9-10 And he said unto me, My grace is sufficient for thee: for my strength is made perfect in weakness. Most gladly therefore will I rather glory in my infirmities, that the power of Christ may rest upon me. 10 Therefore I take pleasure in infirmities, in reproaches, in necessities, in persecutions, in distresses for Christ's sake: for when I am weak, then am I strong.*

Choose to love God, your neighbor, and yourself.

Follow God's rules for a happy life, written in the Bible. Choose to tell the truth, instead of telling a lie. Choose not to steal, instead of taking things from others.

*Matthew 22:37-38 Jesus said unto him, Thou shalt love the Lord thy God with all thy heart, and with all thy soul, and with all thy mind. This is the first and great commandment.*

*Exodus 20:12-17 Honour thy father and thy mother: that thy days may be long upon the land which the LORD thy God giveth thee. 13 Thou shalt not kill. 14 Thou shalt not commit adultery. 15 Thou shalt not steal. 16 Thou shalt not bear false witness against thy neighbour. 17 Thou shalt not covet thy neighbour's house, thou shalt not covet thy neighbour's wife, nor his manservant, nor his maidservant, nor his ox, nor his ass, nor any thing that is thy neighbour's.*

Choose to be kind, instead of being mean.

Choose not to hurt people, instead of hitting or bullying.

Tell your parents, teacher, pastor, bus driver or coach, if you are being bullied.

*Proverbs 6:16-19 These six things doth the Lord hate: yea, seven are an abomination unto him: A proud look, a lying tongue, and hands that shed innocent blood, An heart that deviseth wicked imaginations, feet that be swift in running to mischief, A false witness that speaketh lies, and he that soweth discord among brethren.*

*Ephesians 4:31-32 Let all bitterness, and wrath, and anger, and clamour, and evil speaking, be put away from you, with all malice: 32 And be ye kind one to another, tenderhearted, forgiving one another, even as God for Christ's sake hath forgiven you.*

Choose to be content with what you have, and thankful for what God has given you.

Don't be jealous of what other people have.

Don't always want more and more.

*Leviticus 19:10 And thou shalt not glean thy vineyard, neither shalt thou gather every grape of thy vineyard; thou shalt leave them for the poor and stranger: I am the Lord your God.*

*1 Thessalonians 5:18 In every thing give thanks: for this is the will of God in Christ Jesus concerning you.*

*1 Timothy 4:4 For every creature of God is good, and nothing to be refused, if it be received with thanksgiving:*

*Ephesians 5:20 Giving thanks always for all things unto God and the Father in the name of our Lord Jesus Christ;*

Choose to have faith and believe God will help in all situations, instead of losing faith and giving up.

God really loves you!

*Psalms 27:13-14 I had fainted, unless I had believed to see the goodness of the Lord in the land of the living. Wait on the Lord: be of good courage, and he shall strengthen thine heart: wait, I say, on the Lord.*

*Jeremiah 29:11 For I know the thoughts that I think toward you, saith the Lord, thoughts of peace, and not of evil, to give you an expected end*

*Hebrews 11:1 Now faith is the substance of things hoped for, the evidence of things not seen.*

Choose to have hope,
instead of giving up!

Praise God
for all
good things!

Choose to trust God and let Him
help you overcome obstacles,
instead of letting problems seem so big.

*1 John 3:3 And every man that hath this hope in him
purifieth himself, even as he is pure.*

*Revelation 3:21 To him that overcometh will I grant to sit
with me in my throne, even as I also overcame, and am set
down with my Father in his throne.*

*Psalms 71:5 For thou art my hope, O Lord God:
thou art my trust from my youth.*

*Psalms 71:14 But I will hope continually,
and will yet praise thee more and more.*

Jesus loves all little children,
and He helps you choose good things!

*Luke 18:16-17 But Jesus called them unto him, and said, Suffer little children to come unto me, and forbid them not: for of such is the kingdom of God. 17 Verily I say unto you, Whosoever shall not receive the kingdom of God as a little child shall in no wise enter therein.*

God Really Loves You Book Series™

# GodReallyLovesYou.com

*Matthew 6:9-13 After this manner therefore pray ye: Our Father which art in heaven, Hallowed be thy name. 10 Thy kingdom come. Thy will be done in earth, as it is in heaven. 11 Give us this day our daily bread. 12 And forgive us our debts, as we forgive our debtors. 13 And lead us not into temptation, but deliver us from evil: For thine is the kingdom, and the power, and the glory, for ever. Amen.*

*Matthew 18:3-5 And said, Verily I say unto you, Except ye be converted, and become as little children, ye shall not enter into the kingdom of heaven. Whosoever therefore shall humble himself as this little child, the same is greatest in the kingdom of heaven. And whoso shall receive one such little child in my name receiveth me.*

www.ingramcontent.com/pod-product-compliance
Lightning Source LLC
Chambersburg PA
CBHW040122170426
42811CB00124B/1485